DEBBI DOREAN

WEDDING ETIQUETTE

The Ultimate Guide to Weddings and Etiquette, Discover How to Plan and Manage a Memorable Wedding Event of Your Life

Descrierea CIP a Bibliotecii Naționale a României
DEBBI DOREAN
 WEDDING ETIQUETTE. The Ultimate Guide to Weddings and Etiquette, Discover How to Plan and Manage a Memorable Wedding Event of Your Life / Debbi Dorean – Bucharest: Editura My Ebook, 2021
 ISBN

DEBBI DOREAN

WEDDING ETIQUETTE

The Ultimate Guide to Weddings and Etiquette, Discover How to Plan and Manage a Memorable Wedding Event of Your Life

My Ebook Publishing House
Bucharest, 2021

TABLE OF CONTENTS

Introduction	7
Chapter 1: Why Etiquette Is Essential	9
Chapter 2: Who's Doing what	13
Chapter 3: The Wedding Shower	23
Chapter 4: Invitations and Announcements	30
Chapter 5: Who's Paying	40
Chapter 6: Wedding Gifts	46
Chapter 7: Wedding Tipping	59
Chapter 8: Destination Wedding Etiquette	64
Chapter 9: Thank You's	73
Chapter 10: Calling It All Off	79
Conclusion	80

INTRODUCTION

It's your wedding, do it your way and forget about the rest, right? If you plan to make a few people unhappy and quite a few more wondering where your manners are, then that is the way to go.

Although we do not want to think or talk about it, wedding etiquette is essential. At this very important time in your life, you want everyone to know who you are and what kind of life you are planning to live. The way that you present yourself here is the way they will see you as a couple.

Even if you do not care much about what they do and think, it is still essential for you to find a way to make them feel welcome into your life.

Not to Worry, It's Not Hard!

The hardest part of wedding etiquette is learning about it. That you will do here. The easy part is doing it. There are very few things that are too hard to accommodate. Besides, a wedding is all about pomp and circumstance, so why not lay it all out there?

Wedding etiquette may seem like a difficult process but once you learn a few facts about it and how to easily execute it, you will be well on your way to pleasing your guests, your parents and even find yourself enjoying it all!

So you want to learn about proper wedding etiquette? In this ebook, you will learn all sorts of important things about etiquette and how it affects each one of the people that are in your wedding, come to your wedding and remember your wedding.

By taking the time to follow a few simple rules, everyone can find a place in your wedding memory book.

The goods news is that you will learn a lot about all sorts of aspects of wedding etiquette that you may not have known about. In many ways, you may find yourself wondering about if you should do that or if you should do this. The goal is to provide you with the information you need to make a proper decision about your wedding.

CHAPTER 1

WHY ETIQUETTE IS ESSENTIAL

It's your wedding, do it your way and forget about the rest, right? If you plan to make a few people unhappy and quite a few more wondering where your manners are, then that is the way to go.

Although we do not want to think or talk about it, wedding etiquette is essential. At this very important time in your life, you want everyone to know who you are and what kind of life you are planning to live. The way that you present yourself here is the way they will see you as a couple.

Even if you do not care much about what they do and think, it is still essential for you to find a way to make them feel welcome into your life.

Not To Worry, It's Not Hard!

The hardest part of wedding etiquette is learning about it. That you will do here. The easy part is doing it. There are very few things that are too hard to accommodate. Besides, a wedding is all about pomp and circumstance, so why not lay it all out there?

Wedding etiquette may seem like a difficult process but once you learn a few facts about it and how to easily execute it, you will be well on your way to pleasing your guests, your parents and even find yourself enjoying it all!

Worries Relieved

Another benefit of following the right etiquette for your wedding is that you can avoid problems like these:

- You forgot to invite someone to your wedding and now, they are upset with you!
- You do not know how to properly announce your wedding. Should you put it in the newspaper or send an announcement in the mail?
- Who should you invite to your wedding shower?

- Is it okay to do a gift registry for your wedding? If so, should you put expensive items on it? Does it imply that you want gifts?

- What should you do about guests that are out of town? Is it up to you to provide for them?

- Who's going to pay for what? Should your bridesmaids pay for their dresses? Should you fork over the money for gifts?

- Who should throw your bridal shower?

- Is email an acceptable form of thank you notes for your gifts?

There are plenty of things that are big 'ifs' and since most of us only get married one time, it is rather difficult to actually determine what the right way to go is.

That's why you need to take some time now to determine what the right way to handle these and other circumstances for your wedding is. When you handle them correctly, no one has hurt feelings, has to do too much and you don't look bad.

Wedding etiquette also shows respect and understanding for others. By doing what you can to provide for these things, you show those that you are inviting how much you really do care for them.

Getting Started

While it may be hard to get started with learning about wedding etiquette, it does not have to be. Here are some steps and tips to follow.

- Use this guidebook to insure you meet all the necessary requirements.
- If you question something along the way that is not provided here, use your best judgment to make the right decision.
- Make sure that in the end, it is you that comes out ahead of the game!

Now, let's start learning about wedding etiquette!

CHAPTER 2

WHO'S DOING WHAT?

The first thing that needs to be figured out is who will be handling what aspects of your wedding day.

This is often a difficult situation because people will go one of two ways.

- They may want to do anything and everything for you. They may want to pay for everything, spoil you rotten and make sure that everything is perfect for you. They often want a controlling hand in the wedding planning to go along with this, though.

- They may instead want to play a minimal role in your wedding, making sure that you pay for and lead the way in your wedding decisions.

Of course, you are looking for the happy medium here. To make sure that this happens, the first thing that you need to do is to get together those that will play a large role in your wedding celebration and planning including those that do want to play a role and those that are close family.

This would include:

- Parents, step parents, and grandparents.
- Siblings.
- Godparents or mentors within the family or friend structure.
- Close friends.
- The wedding party.

When everyone can come together, they can make decisions as a whole or at least find out what role they will play in this very important day for you and for them. Now, who's doing what?

The Wedding Etiquette Breakdown of Who's Who

Here's a breakdown of some of the most important players and what they are traditionally supposed to do on your wedding day.

Mother of the Bride

#1 goal is to make sure that the bride's wishes are carried out the way that she wants them to be. The mother of the bride is there to help her to make sure that what she wants and what she needs happens.

It is very important that the mother of the bride allows for the bride's tastes, desires and needs to be provided for. This does not mean that they can dictate what happens, but rather should insure that what does is what the bride wants.

As one of the largest role players, here are her responsibilities:

- **The Wedding Attire.** The mother of the bride should help to find the perfect dress for the wedding, including undergarments and accessories. Not your tastes, but hers should come through.

- **Guest Lists.** The mother of the bride should help to organize guest lists, coordinating with the mother of the groom. If the mother of the groom does not contact her, she should make the first attempt.

- **Help the bride and groom determine their wedding budget.** While she should not do all the work, she should help them allocate where money is going and what are the important aspects to consider.

- **Out of Town Guests.** Those guests that are coming from out of town on the bride's side of the family should be well taken care of by the mother of the bride.

Arranging accommodations and transportation for them is her responsibility. Often this can be minimized if a block of rooms is available to guests at the local hotels as needed by the mother of the bride.

- **Wedding Gowns.** You will select your wedding dress first, but you need to immediately tell the mother of the groom what style and color it is so that she can match or coordinate hers with yours.

- **Wedding Ceremony**. The mother of the bride will need to insure that all the direction for the wedding is given and understood. Where will people stand, sit and how it all will happen are just a few of these concerns. Insure that the receiving line is set up properly as well.
- **Hostess**. As the mother of the bride, you are the hostess of the reception. Have someone help you to plan and execute it.

Mother of the Groom

The mother of the groom has a fine line when it comes to the planning and executing of the wedding. There are some very important things that she should do, but her role is largely dictated by the role that her son and her soon to be daughter in law encourage her to play.

Here are some of her responsibilities according to etiquette.

- **The most important role is to congratulate**. The mother of the groom should call the bride's parents and congratulate and introduce herself to them.

    Announcing how happy she is for the couple, she may want to invite them to dinner at her home or out to a special dinner. A formal get together or an informal one, it is important to get together with them.

- **The Guest List.** The mother of the groom should work with the bride and groom to determine what the right amount of guests should be. Should there be a limit; the groom's mother should insure that she meets this limit. Providing a complete and accurate guest list quickly is essential.

- **The Dress.** The mother of the bride should select her gown first. The mother of the groom should match hers in style and in color. While it does not have to be exactly the same, it should coordinate. It should not match the bride or the bridesmaids.

- **Out of Town Guests.** The mother of the groom should provide for out of town guests that are on the groom's side. Making accommodations and transportation available to them is her job.

- **The Rehearsal Dinner.** The mother of the groom is responsible for the hosting of the rehearsal dinner. She should invite everyone that plays a role in the ceremony and should at least include his or her significant other. Children may also be invited. As for the type of dinner that it is, this is up to her. She can select an informal get together or a more elaborate dinner.

- **Introduce the family and friends on the groom's side to the bride and her mother.** This is usually done in the reception line.

The Maid Of Honor

As maid of honor, you have a special role and place in the wedding. You will insure that the bridesmaids are doing what they should and you set the tone for them. You also should insure that the wedding fits the bride's plans.

Here are some of the tasks that proper wedding etiquette says that the maid of honor should perform.

- *Wedding invitations.* The maid of honor should help to address and send the invitations as well as any announcements.

- *Host the shower.* The maid of honor should throw a party in honor of the couple. This may be the bridal shower. They should work with others in the family for planning and executing this very important event.

- Attend all parties and other pre nuptial events.

- Help the bride throughout the ceremony including help with her train, the receiving line, holding the bride's bouquet during the ceremony, witness the ceremony and sign the marriage certificate, and to carry the groom's ring until needed, unless best man does this.
- *Help the bride to dress.* Assist in her dressing as well as with the other bridesmaids. Help her to undress after the wedding.
- Assist the flower girl with directions and insure she performs her role effectively.
- Help the bride to leave the reception and to have her luggage packed for going away plans.
- Have her wedding dress taken care of including cleaning and preserving as per the wishes of the bride.

Best Man

The best man plays a large role in the wedding as well. Here are some of his responsibilities.
- Provide for the marriage license. He needs to make sure the groom has it!

- Provide the minister's fee to the minister. The groom should give it to him.
- Travel arrangements. The best man should provide for travel arrangements to each destination. He should also provide all the necessary help for planning a honeymoon too.
- Gets the groom to the church.
- Helps the groom to dress for the wedding. He should also help the ring bearer and other groomsmen do the same. The best man should help to insure the ring bearer is taken care of.
- Organize and monitor groomsmen. Insure they are where they are supposed to be on time.
- Provide for any errands that need to be done. The best man should coordinate with the bride's mother and the couple to make sure that they have all that is needed.
- Makes the first toast at the wedding reception. He should also be the first to arrive at the reception and greets guests and the bride and groom when they arrive.
- Acts as a host throughout the day, helping anyone that needs it.

- Helps the groom and bride to leave with the maid of honor's help.
- The best man should also take the tux for himself and the groom back to the rental location. He should take care of the cleaners if the tux is to stay with the groom.
- Has flowers delivered for the bride and the groom on their honeymoon.
- He also signs the marriage certificate as a witness.

These are the main players in the wedding. It is necessary to insure that anyone that wants to be included do so as long as the bride and groom agree to it. Following these wedding etiquette steps will help to keep things organized and keep people from having feelings hurt.

CHAPTER 3

THE WEDDING SHOWER

The wedding shower is a very important part of the entire wedding planning session. Wedding etiquette has some pretty strong advice for those that are having one as well.

There are several key elements to remember here.

- You do not want to sound like you are having a shower to get gifts.//
- You do not want to throw your own shower as a method of getting funds either.
- You do want to celebrate your engagement and upcoming life together.

So, how do we do it?

There are several ways to look at wedding shower etiquette. Let's break it down here.

Who's throwing it?

The first important aspect of the wedding shower is who will actually throw it. You should not throw your own shower, regardless. This is impolite and seems to say that everyone should give you gifts.

It is also impolite in most cultures throughout the United States for your mother to throw your shower as well. In fact, another close family member including your sister should not throw the shower for you.

But, if your sister is your maid of honor, it is acceptable for her to do this.

Who should do it then? Your maid of honor is responsible for hosting a wedding shower for you. It may be a surprise or it may be a large, formal get together.

As the bride, you really should not play a role in its planning other than offering opinions as suggested. This is a way for those that love you to show you so. In fact, it is often something they should plan from start to finish on their own.

More Etiquette to Consider

There are many more little things that factor into the wedding shower's etiquette rules. Consider each one of these if you are to have a proper shower!

- Only people that are invited to your actually wedding or reception should be invited to the wedding shower. For this reason, the maid of honor or who ever are hosting the shower may need to contact the mother of the bride for planning.

The only exception to this is when you are throwing an office wedding shower. These are generally given to you by friends in the office; on their own. The wedding party does not need to play a role in the wedding shower here.

- It is acceptable for you to have several wedding showers. If you have one for each side of the family, that is fine as long as you stick to the rules here. But, it is much more commonly accepted that a family wedding shower will include both the bride and the groom's family. It is a time to get to know each other as well.

- The mother of the bride as well as the maid of honor should try to attend all wedding showers. They do not and should not bring a gift to all of them though. It is acceptable if they do not make it to an office wedding shower.

- Men can be invited to a wedding shower. Generally, men that will be there include fathers of the bride and groom, the best man and the groom himself. But, in some cultures, it is acceptable to have a larger shower that incorporates others as well.

- Only invite a guest to one shower. They should not be asked to come to more than one because they may feel obligated to bring two gifts.

- Those that have been married before can have a second wedding shower. There are no restrictions to this, but they may want to request no gifts if they already have most of what they need to start their new life. Often, the host can request donations for a trip or simpler items instead.

- Most wedding showers should be a surprise to the bride and the groom. While this is not necessary all the time, most brides and grooms do expect to have a wedding shower thrown for them.

Where's it going To Be?

The next big question is where to host the wedding shower. The good news is that there are no guidelines here. You can throw a wedding shower that is over the top formal with live entertainment and lots of food. Or, you can throw an informal get together.

The location of the wedding shower should be depicted by the style of the wedding shower, from informal to extravagant.

Insure that there is enough seating for all the guests. There should be enough room for gifts to be opened including tables for them to be stacked on.

The host of the wedding shower should provide for the means to record what is being given to the bride and groom in a notebook. It is also necessary for the host to welcome guests and greet them at the door.

A Wedding Shower Generally Entails:
- A greeting by the maid of honor, host and the mother of the bride.

- A wedding shower should include a meal of some sort. It can be as simple as a buffet or cold cuts or as complex as a formal dinner.

- The shower should provide comfortable tables for the guests to relax on. Assigned seating is generally not necessary in an informal wedding shower but can be used in a formal.

- The shower should provide for refreshments including a cake or other deserts.

- Most of the time there is some form of music, but generally it is not live entertainment.

- The opening of the presents is generally held after a meal is provided to the guests.

- The bride and the groom should walk around and talk to everyone, thanking them for coming and chatting with guests.

- The wedding party should be thanked by the bride and the groom before or after dinner is served.

- Afternoon wedding showers are the most popular, although they can be held at any time of the day. Weekends are the most common.

More Information

The wedding shower is a wonderful tradition. It is designed to help the new couple to get started on the journey of their lives. The gifts that are given are symbolic of providing the things they will need to have a good start.

Another customary thing that can be done at a wedding shower is for the bridesmaids to collect the ribbons from all presents that are open. These are placed together to create a bouquet that the bride will use in place of the real thing at her wedding rehearsal.

One of the other bridesmaids should take diligent notes about what has been given and who gave it. This will allow the bride to write thank you notes later.

Finally, the planning of a wedding shower should be done well in advance. The more formal that it is the more planning will be needed. Most of the time the shower will happen about one month before the actual wedding takes place. If this is not possible, a wedding shower can occur days before the wedding or even after the honeymoon.

CHAPTER 4

INVITATIONS AND ANNOUNCEMENTS

Wedding etiquette is essential when it comes to letting the world know about your new upcoming marriage and the invitations that you send to your guests. Getting this right really does set the stage for what your guests will think and feel about you for the next months.

Wedding Invitation Design

One of the first things to determine is how the wedding invitation will be set up. Whose name goes first? What happens when things are more than just a simple wedding? The fact is that there are many questions that come up with the wedding invitation design.

First, here are a few etiquette friendly methods of writing an invitation:

- Start with the sponsor or the bride's parents names. "Mr. and Mrs. Bob Smith" should be the beginning of the invitations.

- Follow this with, " request the honor of your presence at the marriage of their daughter"

- Next, include the first names of the bride and the groom, " Ann Marie to Mr. Adam Jones"

- Follow this with the date and time of the wedding followed by the location.

The invitation should also include the groom's parents if both will be helping to pay for or sponsor the wedding. The bride's parent's names should be first, followed by the groom's.

If the bride and the groom are sending the invitations, their names should appear such as this:

Miss Ann Marie Smith And
Mr. Adam Jones

Now, it gets a bit trickier when you add in the divorces and other complications. To determine what the right way to design the wedding invitation is, remember this.

The parents that are issuing the invitations, sponsoring the wedding, paying for the wedding should have their name go first. If you have more than one parent, start the invitation with the bride's parents (father first) and then the groom's parents second.

There are also special situations that can follow these rules such as brothers and sisters hosting the wedding, grandparents and many, many more. The goal is to give proper respect to the individuals that are sponsoring the wedding first and foremost.

List the purpose of the invitation on it. For example, this should be an invitation to the marriage of their daughter or, an invitation to the celebration of their daughter's marriage for a reception only. If there is no reception or only selected guests will be there, the invitation would be directed as an invitation for the ceremony of marriage of the daughter.

Include These Things in the Invitation:

- The name of who is sponsoring the wedding.

- The names of those getting married. The bride's surname may be left out but the groom's should be included. If you use Miss at the beginning of her name, her surname should also be included.

- The date of the wedding, include the day of the week with the date. It is proper to do this several ways including, "Saturday, the tenth day of June," or "Saturday, June tenth," as you see fit. The year can be eliminated or included.

- There should not be any abbreviations used in the invitation, excluding Mr. and Mrs. Do not abbreviates drive, street, or the state.

- No punctuation is used at the ends of sentences. You should use a comma to separate the city and state.

- After the date is listed, the next line should include the time of the event. This too should be spelled out. Do not use am or pm, but if the timing is not obvious, then you can add in "in the morning" for a sunrise wedding or "in the evening" for a sunset wedding.

- This should be followed by the location of the wedding. List the name of the location, Grace Church. On the following line is the church's address. You do not always have to include the address, especially if it is a church. You should include it if the wedding is being held at someone's home, though. People can easily find this information on maps included with the invitation or by a simple internet search.

What Else Goes In The Envelope?

If you have every received an invitation, you know that there are more pieces to it than just this. The method that you use is up to you, but in a traditional wedding, you will want to follow these guidelines.

Reception Card

The reception card is a small sized card that is included to provide the details of the wedding reception to the guests.

If you do not plan to provide this separately, it is important for you to include the reception information on the actual invitation. This is appropriate when the reception is being held at the same location. If not, you really do need to send a separate reception card.

The reception card should include the location of the reception and the time that it is being held. These may then be sent to just individuals that are invited to the reception while you send invitations to the ceremony for others that are not invited to the reception.

Response Cards

You should include response cards in your wedding invitations for your own sanity! Often, receptions will entail the cost per plate, so you will need to know how many guests will be coming to your wedding.

The response cards should state that the guests will or will not be coming as well as request the number of individuals coming. A common way to do this is to use this method:

The Favor of Your Reply Is Requested
_**Will be attending the reception.**
_**Will not be attending the reception.**
_**Number of guests in attendance Please reply by May 10th**

You can change this as long as it includes the necessary information. If you are providing response cards with your invitation, you should provide a self addressed envelop that is stamped with it. The response card should be filled out and sent back to those that are sponsoring the wedding.

If you decide that you do not want to use a response card, you can also use an R.S.V.P. You can add this to the bottom of your invitation or your reception card. Make sure to direct the guests to call a specific number by a specific date.

Often, it can be helpful to use one family member from either side of the family to gather these responses to allow for a more favorable response from the guests. They are more likely to respond to someone they know rather than someone they do not.

If you will be adding this to the invitation itself, keep it in the corner and only do so if the invitation remains uncluttered.

A master list of all those that are invited should be kept on hand. Once the individual's that are invited respond, their name on the list should include how many are coming to the reception and to the ceremony.

This way, the right plans can be made based on however many are coming. It is necessary to contact those that do not respond, especially when the reception is a per plate affair to find out if they are coming.

Design Touches

There are many ways that you can personalize your wedding invitation. The design of your invitation should be a direct reflection of the type and class of the ceremony and reception to follow. If the reception is informal, then there is no need for an elaborate invitation. It will simply confuse guests.

Yet, if the reception is a black tie event, it is necessary to insure that everyone realizes this through the eloquence of the invitation itself. If you are concerned that they may not know that the wedding is a black tie event, add a small notation of it in the corner of the invitation.

You can have your wedding invitation hand drawn or have your local print shop take care of it. If you love calligraphy or a special design, go for that.

There are excellent wedding invitation companies you can work with on the web as well. Make sure to book with them early on so that you have enough time to get your invitations done correctly and out at least a month in advance of your wedding.

The wedding invitation should go out 4-6 weeks prior to the wedding celebration itself. If the reception is a separate event, held on a separate day, there should be two separate invitations sent out in a timely fashion.

Announcements

Announcements can and should be sent out by the parents of the bride or the parents of the groom, or both. This usually serves as a pre cursor to a wedding invitation. An announcement can be placed in the newspaper as well to serve as a way of announcing the happy union. It is essential that an announcement be kept rather formal.

Who to Invite

The next tricky thing to consider about the wedding and the reception is who to invite. While this is completely up to the person that is paying for the wedding, it is customary that all family be invited. Anyone that is a mentor or has played a role in the bride or the groom's life in a significant way should be invited.

It is very important for the bride and the groom to have those around them that they love and cherish. This includes step parents and divorced relatives. While it may not be something that everyone would like, it is necessary to provide this ability to the guests.

For co workers, it is not necessary to invite them unless they are more than just a co worker, such as being a friend. The boss can and should be invited, but do not be offended if they turn you down.

Anyone that has been invited to the wedding shower should be invited. The wedding guest list should be made before that of the wedding shower list to insure there are no mistakes here.

If someone does not have something to do directly with the bride or the groom, or their parents, it is not necessary or obligatory to invite them. The size of the nuptials can also limit how many should be invited. Both families should be considered fairly, though.

CHAPTER 5

WHO IS PAYING?

Who is footing the bill for a wedding is generally a hot topic among brides, grooms and their parents. While traditionally speaking the bride's parents are to pay for the wedding, this is generally falling by the wayside as couples pay their own way.

The wedding budget is something that simply must be worked out well before the wedding plans are underway. In fact, those that are likely to be paying for the wedding, including the parents of the bride and groom, should sit down and have a frank discussion about what their expectations and abilities are.

The budget can be a direct amount or can be broken down line by line. In either case, the goal is to provide the couple with guidelines to know just how much is expected to be paid by who throughout the course of the wedding.

Once you set the date, set a date to talk money. It is the most essential thing to do to insure that everyone is on the right track.

Where etiquette is concerned, though, there are some guidelines that should be followed. Yet, you may be surprised to find that the father of the bride is not the only person that is to be paying for the wedding. In fact, it now includes the groom's family and the couple themselves!

Decisions, Decisions

One of the first things that should be discussed is the overall style of the wedding. Do the bride and the groom want a formal, lavish wedding? If so, to what extreme do they want it to be? If not, do the bride and groom want an informal wedding? Again, to what extreme do they want to take this? Determining the level of hopes that are there is essential to knowing how much will likely is spent.

Also, as much as mom and dad want to, they should not force a style of wedding onto the couple, especially if they will not be footing the entire bill for it.

The Break Down

You can still follow etiquette guidelines especially when the wedding budget is being broken down by those that are in it. Here are some of the things that should be paid for and who should pay for them.

The Bride's Family

Here are some of the things that the bride's family should be paying for. They have by far the most to pay for. This should come from the parents of the bride or someone else that is sponsoring them.

- The wedding gown, the headpiece and the accessories for the bride to wear
- The bridesmaid's bouquet
- Corsages for the grandmothers
- Flowers for the reception and the ceremony
- Arches for the altar
- Canopy, carpeting, kneeling benches, candelabras for the wedding ceremony

- All rented items for the wedding ceremony and the reception
- Invitations, announcements and the production of them
- Napkins, wedding programs and other printed items
- The fees for the church including the musician
- The reception hall fees
- Catering for the reception and any other professional services required during the reception
- Wedding photography, videos, and the music at the reception
- The wedding cake and the wedding favors
- Brunch or lunch for the wedding party

The Groom

The groom traditionally pays his own way throughout the wedding. This may be helped by the groom's family more commonly today.

- Wedding ring for the bride
- Wedding gift for the bride

- Gifts for the ushers or groomsmen
- The bride's bouquet
- The mother's corsages
- Boutonnieres for the groom and the groomsmen
- The marriage license
- The fee for the official doing the wedding
- Limousine services
- Honeymoon arrangements
- All accessories for the groomsmen

The Bride

The bride too is supposed to handle some costs for the wedding.

- The wedding ring for the groom
- The wedding gift for the groom
- Bridesmaids gifts
- Bridesmaids luncheon

The Groom's Family

They help with the following needs

- Groom's cake
- Rehearsal dinner

Other Important Elements

- Bachelor Party is held by the best man
- Bridesmaid's gowns are paid for by the bridesmaids, including the maid of honor
- The groomsmen's formal wear is paid for by the groomsmen including the best man and the fathers.
- Formal wear for the children in the wedding is provided by their parents

CHAPTER 6

WEDDING GIFTS

Wedding gifts are confusing. How much should be spent? Who should buy a gift for the couple? What should be done when the couple already has what they need to start their lives?

There are plenty of things to wonder about, but wedding etiquette dictates what you should and should not do when it comes to wedding gifts.

Whether you are on the receiving side or the giving side, it is essential that this touchy situation gets handled appropriately.

When Gifts Are Given

Wedding gifts are given at various times during the course of the wedding planning and ceremonies. If you are giving the gift, you should know when it is appropriate to give a gift to the bride and groom at each of these times.

- *The engagement party-* if there is an engagement party, small tokens can be given to the bride and the groom. Certainly a card is encouraged, but it is not necessary to go overboard with gifts here. Since this party is reserved for just the most intimate of guests, this can be handled individually as well.

- *The wedding shower-* The most common time to give a gift is at the wedding shower. We will get more into details about the wedding shower in just a minute. For the most part, you should only attend the shower if you are bringing a gift or something sentimental for the couple.

- *The wedding-* If you attend the wedding shower, you do not need to provide another gift for the wedding. But, it is customary to provide a monetary gift to the bride and groom at the wedding, to help them to pay for the wedding and to start off their life together.

The wedding gift, if given should be something of personalized or sentimental value for this special occasion.

Sometimes, the bride's family or close friends may give the bride or the groom something during odd times during the wedding preparations. For example, the maid of honor, a sister of the bride or the mother of the bride, may purchase a keepsake book for them to record their planning adventures.

This is not something that is necessarily required, but can provide sentimental value that can be used throughout the planning of the wedding itself.

Wedding Shower Gifts

When it comes to the wedding shower, gifts are almost a must. While there is no restriction that you should never go to a wedding shower without a gift, it is somewhat assumed that you will.

The gifts given at a wedding shower are designed to help the bride and the groom to begin their life together. For that reason, the gifts given are generally things for their household. You may give them things for the kitchen, the bath, the bedroom or any place else in the home that you know that they need something for.

If you are not sure what the bride and groom need for their new home, it is okay to ask the bride's parents or the groom's parents, or other close family members for advice.

You can give a monetary gift for the wedding shower if you feel that this is a more appropriate gift for the couple. Often, a monetary gift will be one of the most appreciated gifts given at any time simply because of the sheer cost of the wedding itself.

Yet, it is important to take note in the fact that a gift that is given at a wedding shower is the most customary thing given, and the most prized.

At the wedding shower, it is also customary that these gifts will be open for the guests to see. For that reason, gifts should be purchased with this kept in mind.

Other Appropriate Times

The co workers of the bride may decide to give the bride an office shower. At the office shower, those that know the bride well will give her a gift. Generally speaking the gifts are something for the home. But, they are often much less costly than the gifts given at a bridal shower.

The office shower is less formal, generally only being a 'lunch hour' occasion. There should also be a cake and/or a deli tray presented to those that come to the shower. The person closest to the bride will give her the shower but a boss can do so as well.

Guests invited to an office bridal shower do not have to be invited to the wedding shower and do not need to be invited to the wedding unless it was originally planned.

Appropriate Choices

Gifts at a wedding shower can be virtually anything that is needed for the home. While every family is different, gifts are usually given that are high in quality, something that is useful or something that has sentimental value.

The goal of the gift is to help the couple to prepare their new home for their arrival. For that reason, virtually anything for the home, from dishes and pots and pans to fine china and large appliances are acceptable.

Those that are closer to the bride and the groom generally will give a larger gift, but there is no hard rule for this either.

It is customary for the maid of honor and other bridesmaids to give gifts to the bride and groom as well. In most cases, the parents of the couple will also provide a gift to them at this occasion, unless they feel that it is necessary to keep it to themselves, in which case they can.

From The Other Point Of View

If you are the bride or the groom, you too have gifts to give out to those that are in your wedding party. It is customary for these gifts to be given, but what you give is really up to you and your budget. Wedding gifts are a sign of thank you, of welcome to our new life and of a significant start to the new life that you will be leading together.

Gifts for Groomsmen

Traditionally, the groom is responsible for providing some sort of thank you gift to the groomsmen in his wedding party. This does not necessarily need to be of high cost. It is commonly something that has an engraved message or has some value to it.

It is often appropriate to give a gift to the groomsmen that fit with the sense and relationship that the groom has with those individuals. For example, a groom may give a beer mug to his friend, an usher, as a token of appreciation and a tool to remember their friendship over the last years.

The gifts for the groomsmen can be presented to the groomsmen at the rehearsal dinner. If not, they can be presented by the groom to his groomsmen on the wedding day, as the men are preparing and getting ready for the day. It is also appropriate for the gifts for the groomsmen to be given out at the bachelor party if this occurs in the right manner for doing so.

The gift should be something that is worth something as it is a token of thanks and gratitude to the groomsmen for all that they have done to help the groom in preparation of this day and for serving next to him throughout it.

Gifts for the Bridesmaids

Typically, the bride should provide a gift of thanks to her bridesmaids. The gift selection is completely open to what she selects. It is often something significant, though not necessarily costly.

The appropriate gift for the bridesmaids can be chosen as something that is the same for all those in the wedding party. Or, the gifts can be individual items given as a specific gift to each person. This is done at the discretion of the bride herself.

Since the gift is a token of thanks, it should be given as something that is meaningful to the ladies or something that is of value. They will use it as a way to remember this day and the bride.

The gifts for the bridesmaids are generally presented to the bridesmaids by the bride at the rehearsal dinner. They can also be given to the bridesmaids at the bridal luncheon where the bride hosts her bridesmaids for a meal together. If neither of these times is appropriate, the bride can give her bridesmaids a gift as they are preparing for their special day. But, often this is not the best choice as it can be very busy and stressful as it is.

Gifts to Guests

It is also necessary and etiquette dictates that the bride and groom, or those that are hosting the wedding reception and bridal shower, to give the guests that come a gift. This gift is often called a wedding favor.

A wedding favor is presented to the women that attend the event. While it is customary that the favors be given to all females in attendance, if the gift is something that is highly costly or inappropriate, a child can be given an alternative gift in lieu of the larger one.

The wedding favor can be any small token of thanks. There are plenty of wedding sites that offer a variety to select from right on the web. Selection of the wedding favor is completely up to the person hosting the wedding or shower.

Typically, the wedding favor will cost only a few dollars each. They should be marked with a tag that has the date of the event, the name of the couples and the occasion listed on it. Often, a small bouquet of candy is also included with the wedding favor.

Another tradition that is often used is the gift of cigars to the men that attend the wedding reception. The groom or the groom's father is to give one to each man that comes to the reception. It is a sign of welcoming the groom to manhood.

Other Gifts

There are other gifts that can be given throughout the nuptials. Gifts of sentimental value are often exchanged from mother to daughter and from grandmother to granddaughter. Also, fathers may give their son's something to honor the occasion.

While these gifts are not mandatory, they are often done as a token for the parents to honor their child's accomplishments and successes.

Gift Do's and Don'ts

Gifts should never be mentioned on any wedding invitation that is given out by the bride's parents, the groom's parents or the bride and groom. Gifts should not be expected at any time either.

Any gifts that are given should not be opened or used until after the couple has been married. Gifts should remain kept away until after the wedding ceremony.

If the wedding is called off, the gifts should be returned to those that have given them. It is often necessary to keep a record of who gave what to insure that this is easily done should the couple not stay together.

If a wedding is postponed indefinitely, gifts should be returned to the guests. If the wedding is postponed and a date is given, gifts may be kept but should never be opened or used until after the couple is actually married and living together.

Those that have been married in the past can still have a wedding shower thrown for them. It is often a necessary thing just as much as those that have not been married before. Depending on how large the wedding will be should determine how formal and lavish the wedding shower is and therefore the gifts that are given to the bride that has been married before.

For those that are having a wedding shower and do not need things for the home, especially those that already own homes, it is often appropriate to give a lifestyle gift in place of the standard bridal shower gift? This may include things like gift certifications to spas, hotels, or even favorite restaurants.

Other appropriate gifts in this type of situation include a vacation package or part of it or a gift of lodging at a bed and breakfast. Other gifts of the same type are most welcome.

Monetary gifts are always appreciated and are more than well used for any type of gift throughout the wedding shower or the wedding itself but monetary gifts may be more costly than the average gift for a bridal shower.

When it comes to gift registries, these are appropriate for the wedding shower. It is now proper etiquette to provide information with the wedding shower invitation about where the bride and the groom are registered for their wedding.

The bride and groom should register for their wedding gifts together. This should be done in several ways. It is appropriate to register at several locations to give guests options to select from. It is also appropriate and necessary to select gifts from all price ranges.

Gifts should be selected based on needs and tastes but should have a complete scope of prices so that no one feels obligated to purchase something that is too costly. On the other hand, those that do want to purchase a very nice gift for the couple should be able to find these items to select from as well.

The bride and groom should not send out invitations to the wedding shower, but it is appropriate for them to fill a gift registry.

Never request that only monetary gifts be given at either the bridal shower or the wedding itself. If this is the preferred method, the host of the wedding shower or the host of the wedding itself should encourage monetary gifts only through word of mouth.

Another option for this situation is to list a honeymoon registry where guests can provide gifts to help with the creation of the honeymoon or the costs of it. A fund can be set up on one of several websites to provide for this need as well.

Returning Gifts

Even with the best of efforts, gifts may be duplicated; the wrong size or it may not be of use to the bride and the groom.

When this happens, it is okay to return the gift and purchase something that is useful instead.

For this reason, gift receipts, which are commonly found today in most department stores, should be provided to the couple. The couple can then make exchanges if they are necessary.

The only exception to this rule is when gifts are given for sentimental value or they are hand made. Then, the gifts should not be returned but displayed.

Do not be offended if the couple does return the gift that is given to them by you. It is more important that they have a gift that is of use to them to remember you by.

CHAPTER 7

WEDDING TIPPING

Wedding etiquette is just like any other type of etiquette when it comes to tipping. If you are given a service, it is essential that you provide a tip to the person that is providing it to you.

Tipping is a way of thanking an individual for a job well done. Therefore, if they do not do a good job or there is some large problem that is not able to be rectified, the tip should be lessened or not provided. But, remember that this is the source of income for the service provider.

So, who do you tip and who is supposed to tip them? Here are some general rules to help you to decide what the right way to handle payment in the form of tips is.

Who to Tip

The first thing to take note of is just who you should be tipping. One rule of thumb for this is to take a look at the final bill. Today, most of the opportunities for tips are often applied right to the final bill.

For example, in most restaurants, a large party will have gratuity added to the bill. But, that does not mean that this is the right amount to tip (it may be too high or too low) and it does not mean that you have to pay for it at that level

If you pay gratuity in the final bill of your service provided for your wedding, should you give a tip on top of this to the service provider?

If you feel that the service provider has gone over and beyond what was expected of them, then it can be appropriate to provide them with more of a tip for your needs. If you feel that the tip is not enough, then by all means, a larger tip can and should be left.

But, Which Services And How Much?

Knowing when to tip is just as important. There are several opportunities that you will have to give a tip at. Here's a breakdown of some you should take note of.

- Those that include a tip already in the final bill may be the caterer, the banquet managers, waiters, bartenders, and bridal consultants. Here, a tip is generally about 15%, but should only be provided if the service is over and beyond the standard since you are already tipping them in the bill.

- **Your Limousine Driver**. You should tip the limo driver for your service. Notice in the contract if there is an amount of gratuity already listed. If so, it is not necessary. If not, or you receive high levels of service, a tip of 15% is appropriate.

- **Photographers, florists and musicians**. If not provided in the contract, a tip in the amount of 15% to 20% is appreciated. Of course much more is for better service.

- **Priests, Rabbis and Clergymen.** This is one tip not to be forgotten as it is not provided elsewhere. The groom should provide a tip to be given by the best man to the official. Commonly, this amount should not be less than $100. While it is a donation, it should always be provided. More should be provided if the official had to drive a long distance.

- **Civil Service.** Since there is no cost set here, it is appropriate to provide a tip of $50 to $100 for the civil servant that is providing the service. Often, there is a suggested donation posted in these offices.

- **Musicians and organists at the ceremony.** These services may have gratuity in the contract, so make sure that you check first. This is only the case if you actually rent the church for use. If not, then a tip should be provided as well. The tip can range form $40 to $75 depending on the amount of service and the quality that is provided.

Tipping should not be something that is forgotten. If the groom can not remember to do the tipping, then the best man should step in. It is necessary to show appreciation and follow proper etiquette for tipping.

CHAPTER 8

DESTINATION WEDDING ETIQUETTE

Destination weddings are very popular. In fact, in some ways, etiquette rules have not yet caught up to the destination theme at all! Yet, when it comes to this type of wedding style, you really do have a lot to think about before you go off to get married.

Destination weddings are weddings in which you will travel to a location other than any place near to you, to be married. These weddings are common in resorts and other fabulous places. Yet, although they are so popular, that does not mean that they are the best choice for everyone, especially those with a large family that is expecting a large celebration of the wedding.

While the ultimate decision about a destination wedding is all up to you, it is common practice to insure that the wedding satisfies everyone's needs. Here are some basic tips that we will expand on later.

Tip One:

Do not expect the world to follow you to your destination wedding. Not many of your guests will be able to afford it, find travel arrangements or get off of work to go. So, expect for some not to be able to come with you for your wedding.

Tip Two:

Send out invitations and 'hold the date' cards to your guest well in advance. Several months should be given if you except them to come so that they can get the proper travel arrangements made including the necessary legal documents if it is out of the country.

Tip Three:

Do something for those that can not make it to your wedding but are close enough to you that want to celebrate your wedding with you at home. For example, you can have your wedding ceremony in Hawaii, but have a reception back at home too for those that could not make it.

Etiquette for the Wedding

There are several things that come into play when it comes to a destination wedding ceremony. The first is the cost. Unlike a traditional wedding ceremony, it is not going to fly for the parents to pay for this type of wedding celebration, especially when most are counting on that big wedding to celebrate your marriage.

So, if you plan to have a destination wedding, plan to sit down and talk to those that will be paying for it. There are many additional costs folded into the wedding itself here.

One benefit to the wedding destination is that most will take care of all of the planning for your wedding for you. They can help you to make arrangements for the ceremony, lodging, foods, and even for legal requirements. This does lessen the amount of planning that you will be required to do, but it may also limit you to what you can do yourself. Depending on the level of comfort you have in giving someone else the ability to handle your wedding, should be a consideration here.

Once you figure out money, determine who is coming.

You will want to invite many people to your wedding ceremony, but you may be limited to those that you can pay to come. Now, not everyone you invite is someone that you are going to have to pay for, but some you may.

Be quite frank with those that you invite about what you are covering in costs and what they will have to. Realize that some may not be able to make it and that should be okay with you. Do not pressure those that have financial or employment strains to come to your destination wedding unless you plan to pay for them to do so.

You should pay for the lodging of your wedding party though. The people that are sponsoring the wedding need to pay for the lodging and the needs of the bridesmaids and the groomsmen. Insure that this is factored into the cost of the wedding itself.

If you will have more guests coming for your destination wedding, make sure that you do everything you can to help them to get the lowest rates. For example, you may be able to arrange group rates or book a block of rooms for them to stay in. While they may be paying for it, this can be more encouragement to those that have not visited the area to come down.

Define the Dress Code

Another thing that is necessary for the host of the destination to do is to help the guests to know what to wear when they get there. There are two things to consider here. First, the attire for the wedding may be different at a destination wedding. If so, it may be necessary to determine what the right attire is and then insure that the wedding party and the guests know what that attire should be.

If they have not traveled to the location before, it is necessary for you to give them help with knowing what the right type of clothing to bring and wear is. This should include clothing for time spent not with the wedding party as well. You should allow your guests to know what the theme, informal or formal, of the wedding ceremony will be. Any other gatherings that happen should also be considered and communicated as well.

What to Do

Another factor to consider about the destination wedding is what should be done during it.

If you will be inviting guests to your destination wedding, make sure you provide enough for them to do when they are there.

The wedding ceremony is only the start of what you should do. You should have a welcoming dinner or cocktail where you will inform the guests, once they arrive what the agenda is. Even if it is limited by just the ceremony and a small reception, this information should be presented to the guests even before they arrive.

Some will want to spend the entire time with you while others will be more responsive to heading out to explore the area on their own. Make sure that as the bride and groom and the parents of them sponsoring the wedding that you cater to their needs here.

It is customary for some meals to be spent with various guests that come to the wedding. Often, these can include dinner each night or it may just be a get together on the beach. Whatever it is, make sure guests are aware of what your plans are for the time that they spend with you.

What to Do Back Home

No matter if three people come or if 103 people come to your destination wedding, there are likely to be those that did not come to it but still would like to celebrate with you. A reception is appropriate and should be given to the bride and groom.

It is acceptable for the bride and the groom to host their own reception following their destination wedding. It is also acceptable for the parents of the bride or the groom, or both to host it. It serves the same purpose as the reception of a standard wedding reception would. The same etiquette settings apply here.

Most commonly, the reception following a destination wedding is somewhat informal. For that reason, it is often important to convey to the guests that are being invited just how formal it will be. Make sure guests know if your wedding reception will be in the backyard or if it will be a formal affair. While either is appropriate, it is necessary to insure that the guests know what is right to wear and to give.

You should not register for a wedding registry for gifts. You should not imply that you want or expect gifts at your wedding reception either. While most guests will bring a card, they may not give a large number of gifts for informal celebrations.

The reception should include anyone that you would like to share your wedding celebration with. It is necessary to insure that guests do not feel slighted if they were not invited to the wedding by allowing them to come to the reception.

Anyone that may not feel comfortable with you having a destination wedding should be talked to, one on one about it. Provide them with information about why you want to have this style of wedding, how it will work and encourage them to come. Insure them that they can come and join you and that you will have a reception to celebrate when you come back as well.

What About The Wedding Shower?

If you are having a destination wedding, one of the most commonly wondered things is if you should have a wedding shower or not. It is not a guarantee that you will have one, since guests should be invited to a wedding shower only if they are invited to the wedding itself.

Yet, if there will be a reception for the wedding when you get back, it may be acceptable. Also, it is necessary for you to insure that you do not have your own wedding shower, or anyone that is paying for your destination wedding. It should be a friend or the maid of honor that hosts your wedding shower.

It is appropriate to have a gift registry for your wedding shower. You should follow the same etiquette guidelines here as you did for a standard wedding shower.

CHAPTER 9

THANK YOU'S

Your wedding is a very important time for you. Of course, it is also one of the most costly events that will happen in your life as well.

Therefore, a big old thank you is appropriate for everyone that does anything for your wedding, little or small, to make it a memorable one.

The list goes on and on and while most people will say that they just want you to be happy, you should provide them all with appreciation in one form or another for what they are doing for you. This goes doubly for parents that are paying for the wedding (and all your desires and quirks!)

There are several important things to remember when it comes to saying thanks. You should be giving these throughout the next year or so in big ways to those that help you through this very stressful time.

Thank You Notes

The first thing that is a big thank you to provide is that of the bridal shower. If you have any type of celebration before this in which you are given gifts or special treatment, thank you notes should also be applied here.

In fact, head to the local stationery store and pick up a lot of thanks you notes. You'll need most of them! Pick out ones that match your wedding invitations or pick out something else. Just have them on hand to send out quickly.

The Wedding Shower

When it comes to the thank you notes that you will be writing for your wedding shower, you need to carefully consider what you are doing here. Here are some very important etiquette tips you need to follow for wedding thank you notes for your shower.

- A personal note is the only way to go. Just telling someone thank you is not enough and is considered very impolite. You need to pen a personal note to them to tell them how grateful you are that they took the time to provide you with this gift.

- Do not send pre printed thank you notes. This is tacky and can give the impression of just being after the gift. You should hand write your thank you notes so you provide your gift givers with a clean appreciation of what their gift has meant to you.

- Your thank you note should mention the type of gift that they gave you. Thanking them for the beautiful china with a pattern that you love is more appropriate and better taken than just saying thanks for the gift. Make sure to personally mention what gifts have been given to you.

- Those that throw the wedding shower for you should also be thanked through a personal, hand written thank you note. If they also provide you with a gift as well as the shower help, then you can thank them for both in the same thank you note.

- Thank your guests quickly for the gifts that they give you. You should send out thank you notes within ten days of your wedding shower. You should send out thank you notes for your wedding gifts within two weeks of returning from a honeymoon. If you get a wedding gift at a different time, then send a thank you note as soon as possible.

- Personalize the thank you note by using this trick. Instead of saying "I" throughout the note, say, "you" in it. This way, the information is provided to your gift giver in a way that shows the value that they have by giving this gift.

- Use black or blue ink to write your thank you notes. This is the best method for doing so as it can provide the clearest reading ability as well as provides for a formal tone.

- If you receive more than one gift from anyone on separate occasions, you should pen two separate thank you notes, one for each. If they give you two gifts on the same day, then both can be included in the thank you note.

- When you address your envelopes, make sure that your new address, if you have one, is what is used on the front, return address. This allows your gift givers to have your new address.

- If more than one person gave you the gift, you should write an individual thank you note for each person. If there are more than ten people that have given you the gift, then one note to all of them is sufficient. This depends on the size and cost of a gift. A very expensive gift should warrant a thank you note for each person regardless.

- Take you time when writing your thank you notes, to make sure that they are neat and well written. It shows that you took the time to care for them and thank them in a personal way.

Wedding Gifts

When your wedding rolls around, you will likely have even more gifts to write thank you notes for. These gifts are likely to be more of a monetary nature though. Yet, any type of gift that you get for your wedding you need to properly take note of.

Wedding gifts of a monetary nature should be thanked in a generic way.

"Thank you so much for your check" or "Thank you so much for your monetary gift" is appropriate here. You should not include the amount of the gift in the thank you note. But, you can tell the person that is sending you the gift what you will use the money for should you have this figured out.

For example, telling them that you are putting the money towards your down payment on a new home is a great way to show them how well spent their money will be.

All gifts given to you at your wedding should receive the same type of personal thank you note. If you are getting something from anyone, provide them with a note of thanks that comes from the heart as it will make many people quite happy.

Make sure to provide thank you notes to all of those that have helped to make your wedding what it is too. This would include those that paid for it and those that helped in your wedding party.

CHAPTER 10

CALLING IT ALL OFF

If you are reading this section, our sympathy goes out to you. Not because you are calling off your wedding, but the tasks that are ahead of you from this front. It is not easy to call on those that you were talking about being so happy with and telling them that things just did not work out.

But, it is a must to do. The good news is that if you find yourself in a position to call off your wedding, you can get some others to help you to handle this situation.

More than likely, you are in no mood to be telling the world your story as to why it just did not work out. You may even be a bit overwhelmed with how to do this the right way. One step at a time is how you will get through it.

By the way, we do mean both of you since the groom and the bride are responsible for calling off their wedding.

Here are some things to consider about how you should properly call off your wedding.

No Announcement Sent

If no announcement has been sent out about your wedding just yet, then the word about calling off the wedding can be done by simple word of mouth. In fact, you should only have to tell those that you told yourself.

Announcement Sent

If you or your parents have sent an announcement to your family and friends telling them that you were being engaged, it is important that another formal announcement go out on paper saying that the wedding has been called off.

Newspaper Announcements

If there has been an announcement in the newspaper, then there should be another to say that the nuptials have ended by mutual consent. No blame or details need to be provided.

Wedding Invitations Sent

If the wedding invitations have been sent out inviting people to your wedding, another formal wedding invitation needs to go out, letting everyone know that the wedding has been canceled.

Close To the Wedding Day

If the wedding day is fast approaching, it is imperative that guests be called and told about the called off state of events. The first ones to be called are traveling guests. You should allow everyone to know that things just have not worked out the best and leave it at that. Do not feel you need to elaborate because things just get twisted here.

Postponing the Wedding

If you have to postpone the wedding, you can do this following the same rules as above. But, you will want to tell your guests just what has caused the delay in this case. Whether it be illness or a death, they are likely to understand if you tell them in time.

If you know when the new wedding will take place, that information can be included. If you do not, another invitation will need to be sent out when the time does come to inform guests. Do not have a second wedding shower, though.

Calling Off the Wedding after the Wedding Shower

If you have had your wedding shower and you are now canceling your wedding, you will need to take some important steps with your guests and the gifts that you received.

The gifts given at a wedding shower are given for the bride and the groom to start their new life. If that is not going to happen, you need to return the gifts to your guest promptly.

You should not open any of your wedding shower gifts until after the bride and groom have been married so as to avoid a problem in this situation. It is often that a gift may need to be returned for other reasons as well.

If you have opened the wedding gift that was given to you, contact the gift giver and arrange to pay back the gift giver for the gift itself. If this is not possible, there should be restitution made in some way.

CONCLUSION

Following proper wedding etiquette is not hard nor is it an option. If you are planning your wedding and would like all of those that are around you be find it to be a wonderful event, then take the notes that you find here to heart.

Wedding etiquette does not have to be too hard to do. If you have questions that are not answered here, you always have the option of finding out the right solution elsewhere or taking a good guess at what it is. When you think of all those that are effected by the decision you will make, then you will find yourself having the right answer ultimately.

Wedding etiquette is also always changing. With more and more events taking place, look for some changes to come to what you think wedding etiquette should be too.